I Can Read!

2 WITH HELP

ALEXANDER HAMILTON
A Plan for America

by Sarah Albee
pictures by Chin Ko

HARPER
An Imprint of HarperCollinsPublishers

Alexander Hamilton was a soldier,
a lawyer, and a financial wizard.
He had a brilliant mind.
George Washington trusted him.

Dear Parent:
Your child's love of reading starts here!

Every child learns to read in a different way and at his or her own speed. Some go back and forth between reading levels and read favorite books again and again. Others read through each level in order. You can help your young reader improve and become more confident by encouraging his or her own interests and abilities. From books your child reads with you to the first books he or she reads alone, there are I Can Read Books for every stage of reading:

SHARED READING
Basic language, word repetition, and whimsical illustrations, ideal for sharing with your emergent reader

BEGINNING READING
Short sentences, familiar words, and simple concepts for children eager to read on their own

READING WITH HELP
Engaging stories, longer sentences, and language play for developing readers

READING ALONE
Complex plots, challenging vocabulary, and high-interest topics for the independent reader

ADVANCED READING
Short paragraphs, chapters, and exciting themes for the perfect bridge to chapter books

I Can Read Books have introduced children to the joy of reading since 1957. Featuring award-winning authors and illustrators and a fabulous cast of beloved characters, I Can Read Books set the standard for beginning readers.

A lifetime of discovery begins with the magical words "I Can Read!"

Visit www.icanread.com for information
on enriching your child's reading experience.

To Cassie
—S.A.

To my wife, Sasha. For your patience, love,
endless support, and unfailing sense of humor
while I worked to complete this book.
—C.K.

Picture Credits
The portrait of Elizabeth Hamilton on page 31 is courtesy of the National Archives.
The portrait of young Alexander Hamilton on page 28 is courtesy of the Library of Congress.
Photo of Alexander Hamilton grave site on page 32 courtesy of Jeff Shake.
The following pictures are © Getty Images: page 29, the duel; page 30, painting of enslaved workers on a sugar plantation, portrait of Alexander Hamilton by Thomas Hamilton Crawford; page 31, pair of dueling pistols; page 32, ten-dollar bills.

I Can Read Book® is a trademark of HarperCollins Publishers.

Library of Congress Control Number: 2017956245
ISBN 978-0-06-243291-9 (trade bdg.)—ISBN 978-0-06-243290-2 (pbk.)

Book design by Jeff Shake

20 21 22 LSCC 10 9 8 7 6 5 4

❖   First Edition

But Hamilton was also stubborn
and proud.

His bold ideas angered some people.

Thomas Jefferson disagreed with him.

So did a man named Aaron Burr.

Alexander Hamilton was born
on a tiny British island
in the Caribbean.
His family was poor.
His father ran off,
and his mother died
when Alexander was eleven.

Alexander moved in with friends

and found a job in shipping.

When Alexander was a young teen,
his boss got sick, moved away,
and left Alexander in charge.
The boy ran the business by himself!

When Alexander was seventeen,
a hurricane struck the island.
He wrote a dramatic letter about it
that was published in a newspaper.
Some wealthy men were so impressed
that they sent the boy to college
in America, so he could study law.

There was talk of war with England.

Alexander joined the colonists' side.

He gave speeches and wrote essays.

General Washington heard about
the bright young captain.

He made Alexander his aide.

But Alexander wanted to fight.

Finally, Washington agreed.

Hamilton helped defeat the British

at the Battle of Yorktown.

During the war, Hamilton met
and married Elizabeth Schuyler.
She was the daughter of a general.

After the war, the United States

were not very united.

The war had been expensive.

The government had borrowed money.

How would the war debts be paid?

Americans argued about

money, trade, taxes, and borders.

George Washington became president.
He chose Hamilton to be the first
secretary of the treasury.
Hamilton wanted every state to help
pay the young country's debts.
Like Washington, Hamilton
believed in a good banking system,
a strong national government,
and a well-organized army.
But others disagreed.

Secretary of State Thomas Jefferson
disagreed with Hamilton.
Jefferson thought America's future
should have farms, not factories.
On his own farm in Virginia,
slaves did most of the work.

Hamilton was against slavery.

He planned for banks, factories,

and businesses in America's future.

His planning shaped the new country.

Hamilton created the Coast Guard.
He made plans that helped lower
America's debt.
And he created the US Mint.
(The first coins were made from
Washington's household silver.)

Then Washington stepped aside.

John Adams was elected president.

Hamilton went to New York.

He became an excellent lawyer.

But he kept writing about politics.

In 1800, Thomas Jefferson,

Aaron Burr, and John Adams

all received votes for president.

This time John Adams lost.

But Jefferson and Aaron Burr tied.

Hamilton thought

that Jefferson was a bad choice,

but Burr was worse.

With Hamilton's support,

Jefferson became president.

Then, in 1804, Burr ran
for governor of New York.
At a party, Hamilton said
he did not trust Burr.
He said that Burr was "dangerous."
Burr lost the election.

Burr heard what Hamilton had said.

Burr wrote him an angry letter.

Hamilton refused to apologize.

Burr challenged Hamilton to a duel.

Hamilton and Burr both wanted
to settle their argument with honor.
They thought a duel was the answer.
Hamilton wrote a goodbye letter
to his wife—just in case.

On the day of the duel,

the two men aimed their pistols.

Two shots rang out.

Burr's bullet hit Hamilton.

Hamilton's bullet hit a high branch.

Hamilton fell, badly wounded.

The doctors could do nothing.

Elizabeth hurried to his bedside.

She brought their seven children.

Hamilton died the next day.

He was only forty-nine years old.

Burr did not go to jail,
but his career was ruined.
Hamilton did not live to see
how well his grand plans worked,
but his genius lives on today.

Timeline

1750

1757
Hamilton is born.

1772
The teenager is sent to America.

1760

1773
He enrolls at King's College (now called Columbia University) to study law.

1776
The Declaration of Independence is signed.

1770

1777
Hamilton joins General Washington's staff.

1780
Hamilton marries Elizabeth Schuyler (pronounced SKY-ler).

1781
Hamilton helps defeat the British at Yorktown.

1780

1783
The American Revolution ends.

1787
Hamilton helps write the Federalist Papers.

1789
Washington is elected the first president.
Hamilton is chosen as the first secretary of the treasury.

1790

1795
Hamilton resigns as secretary of the treasury.

1797
John Adams becomes the second president.

1800

1800–1801

President John Adams is not reelected.
Jefferson and Burr are tied.
Hamilton supports Jefferson over Burr.

1801

Burr becomes vice president.
Philip Hamilton, the Hamiltons' oldest child,
is killed in a duel at age nineteen.

1804

Alexander Hamilton
is killed by Aaron Burr
in a duel.

1836

Aaron Burr dies at the age of eighty.

1854

Elizabeth Hamilton dies at the age of ninety-seven.

29

Hamilton's Views on Slavery

As a boy, Alexander Hamilton lived on a tropical Caribbean island.

On the island, wealthy white plantation owners used enslaved people to grow sugarcane.

Alexander witnessed the horrors of slavery.

He opposed slavery for the rest of his life.

Enslaved workers on a sugar plantation.

Hamilton's Essay Writing

Many Americans thought the new country was too big for just one government. They thought each state should be in charge. Hamilton asked James Madison and John Jay to help him write essays to convince people to accept the new Constitution. Their essays were printed in New York newspapers. They were called the Federalist Papers.

Hamilton wrote most of the essays. Hamilton was a great writer. It worked. The Constitution was adopted.

Alexander Hamilton

Hamilton's Family

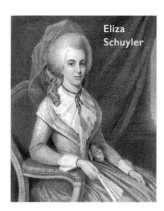
Eliza Schuyler

Alexander's wife, Elizabeth (Eliza) Schuyler, came from a large, wealthy family. She and Alexander had eight children together. Their oldest, Philip, was killed in a duel when he was only nineteen.

After Alexander died, Eliza spent the rest of her life helping the world remember her husband. She died at age ninety-seven. They found Alexander's last letter to her tucked inside her dress.

Hamilton's Death

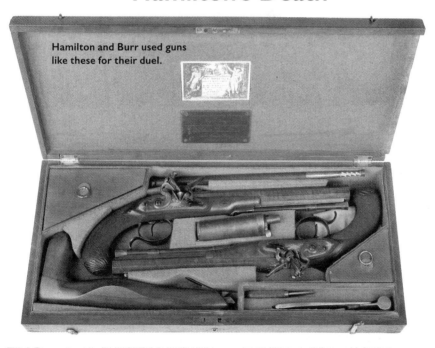
Hamilton and Burr used guns like these for their duel.

Did Burr intend to kill Hamilton, or was it a terrible accident?

Burr was known to have very bad aim.

Did Hamilton intend to shoot way over Burr's head, or did his gun go off as he fell?

We may never know what really happened.

Hamilton's Thoughts About Money

Hamilton created coins that included the dime, the penny, and the half-penny. He thought it was important to have coins worth small amounts, so that people who were not wealthy could buy and sell things.

Today Alexander Hamilton's face is on the ten-dollar bill.

Places to Visit

Hamilton's burial site, New York, NY

The Hamilton Home
The Grange
New York, NY
(*https://www.nps.gov/hagr/planyourvisit/hours.htm*)

Elizabeth Schuyler's Family Home
Albany, NY
(*https://parks.ny.gov/historic-sites/33/details.aspx*)

Alexander and Elizabeth's Burial Place
Trinity Church Cemetery
New York, NY
(*https://www.trinitywallstreet.org*)

Alexander Hamilton's Statue
Outside the US Treasury Building
Washington, DC
(*https://www.treasury.gov/*)